I WOULD RATHER BE HAPPY

Faith Mwende Nthakyo

I WOULD RATHER BE HAPPY

First edition. December 5, 2024.

ISBN: 979-8230271987

Written by Faith Mwende.

Life is too short to be anything but happy.Choose to enjoy every moment and live with purpose.

Happiness is a choice.

When you choose happiness you are choosing a more fulfilled life.

TABLE OF CONTENTS

Dedication

I dedicate this book to my Heavenly Father, in whom I live, move, and have my being. Thank You for Your unfailing love, guidance, and strength to share this journey of joy and self-discovery. All glory and honor belong to You.

To my children, Neema, Jayden and Liana: May you choose to live lives filled with peace, love, and boundless happiness.

Acknowledgment

To my dear husband Paul for your unwavering love and support.

And always encouraging me to think outside the limits society puts on us as women.

To my siblings and friends for their encouragement through the process I am grateful.

Forward

The mantra "do whatever makes you happy" has become an anthem to justify poor decisions. We live in a world that constantly sells us things promising joy and happiness at every turn. We are told we'll find joy if we look a certain way, leading to the emergence of countless products designed to make us "feel" prettier, slimmer, lighter, more voluptuous—for men, the allure is in having longer beards, more money, or more cars, among other things. The scramble and race to "feel happy" is more intense in this day and age than in previous generations, even though we have so much more than they did.

This raises the question: What truly makes you happy? And where does that happiness come from?

In this book, Faith graciously takes us on a journey of self-discovery and helps us unearth the answers to these profound questions. I hope that as you turn each page, your heart will soar with enlightenment and set you on a path toward becoming a better version of yourself.

Irene Nkatha Chege

Introduction: The journey to happiness

Every woman deserves happiness, yet too often, we place it in the hands of others. We wait for our partners, families, or careers to bring us joy, forgetting that happiness is a choice—a gift we give ourselves.

This book is a journey to reclaiming that joy. It's about recognizing the power we have over our happiness and learning how to anchor it in faith, self-love, and the beauty of life itself. Whether you are single, married, or somewhere in between, the lessons here will empower you to create a life filled with peace, laughter, and fulfillment.

As a daughter, wife, mother, and woman of faith, I have lived through my share of challenges and triumphs. Along the way, I have discovered that happiness isn't about perfection or external circumstances—it's about making the conscious decision to live with joy every single day.

Let's walk this path together. Let's embrace the life we were meant to live—a life filled with purpose, gratitude, and unshakable happiness.

Chapter One: Stop postponing your happiness

"I would rather be happy now."

Postponing your joy refers to the tendency to delay happiness or fulfillment until certain conditions are met, such as achieving a specific goal, reaching a milestone, or overcoming a particular challenge. This mindset often creates the belief that happiness is something to be earned or obtained in the future, rather than experienced in the present. It can lead to a cycle of continuous striving, where joy is perpetually postponed and never fully realized in the moment.

In relation to happiness, postponing joy can prevent us from appreciating what we have now and may cause stress, burnout, or feelings of inadequacy. Instead, embracing gratitude and learning to find joy in everyday moments, regardless of external achievements, can lead to a deeper and more consistent sense of happiness.

Growing up, my parents, were very generous,my mum in particular, remains one of the kindest and most giving people I have ever known to date. Imagine this: We were a middle-income family living in Umoja, Nairobi, the houses were modest, mostly two-bedroom units. At the time, we were four siblings, yet we often had one or two cousins living with us.

Despite our limited resources, my parents always found room in their hearts and home for anyone in need. My mom worked for the government, which meant her salary was modest at best. Most of our livelihood depended on my dad's income. We did not grow up in abundance but we were happy with the little we had.

I remember going to school with holes in my shoes. On rainy days, I would slip cardboard into them to prevent my socks from getting soaked. This was not in the rural countryside but right in Nairobi.I had only one set of uniforms, had to wash it every evening after school,if it didn't dry had to iron the them to make them wearable. Yet, despite these challenges, my childhood was filled with immense happiness.

Our home was a place of joy and laughter. We didn't need much to be content. Sitting together as a family, telling stories, and enjoying each other's company was our greatest treasure. My parents fostered an environment of peace and love, teaching us that happiness does not come from material wealth.

When we later moved to a slightly bigger company estate, it was still a simple three-bedroom house. By then, we were five children, yet my parents still welcomed guests—a cousin needing a place to stay or a member of the church with no where to stay. Meals were often simple—githeri or ugali—but the stories shared around our dining table made every meal special.

Looking back, those moments defined my happiest childhood memories,because of the love and fellowship we shared with one another. This taught me a valuable lesson: Happiness doesn't come from things—it comes from within. Many people think, "I'll be happy when I get that car," Or "When I buy a bigger house, I'll finally feel content." But all this things offer only fleeting joy.

I was a banker for 17 years, and working in a bank had its advantages easy access to loans,therefore I was able to buy the things I thought I needed to be happier but I learnt from personal experience and from my customers, that material things—no matter how grand—offer only temporary satisfaction. When you buy that car, there is a lot of excitement but after a while, you want a bigger better car. When you move into your dream house, it feels exhilarating at first, but that feeling fades the longer you stay in that house .

True happiness comes from appreciating what you have, no matter how little. It comes from finding joy in the simplest of things—listening to a great song,a beautiful sunrise, the sound of laughter, a thoughtful phone call from a friend, or even the quiet gratitude of waking up pain-free.

There are several ways in which people tend to postpone or stop their happiness, often without realizing it. These tendencies can arise from societal pressures, self-limiting beliefs, or unaddressed emotional patterns.

1. The "I'll be happy when..." Mindset: Many individuals wait for external circumstances to align before they allow themselves to feel happiness. This might involve waiting for a promotion, financial stability, or a specific achievement. However, this approach often leads to a perpetual state of postponement, where happiness is always tied to future events rather than being experienced in the present moment. According to Sonja Lyubomirsky in her book The How of Happiness, individuals who focus on the present and appreciate small, everyday joys experience greater overall happiness.

2. Perfectionism: Perfectionists often set attainable high standards for themselves and their lives, leading them to feel that they can only be happy once they've achieved a certain level of "perfection." This creates a barrier to happiness, as they never feel good enough. Research by Brené Brown in her work on vulnerability and shame has shown that perfectionism can inhibit the ability to embrace joy and lead to burnout and self-doubt.

3. Chasing External Validation: Constantly seeking approval from others—whether from family, friends, or society—can prevent

individuals from experiencing genuine happiness. This reliance on external validation leaves people feeling unfulfilled, as their happiness is tied to factors they cannot fully control. As Mihaly Csikszentmihalyi discusses in his work on Flow, happiness is more often derived from intrinsic satisfaction and personal fulfillment rather than external approval.

4. Fear of Change: Some individuals resist happiness because they fear it will disrupt their lives or relationships. This can stem from a fear of success, fear of being "too happy," or believing that they don't deserve happiness. Tara Brach, in her book Radical Acceptance, notes that the fear of change or success often stems from deep-rooted feelings of unworthiness, which can hold people back from embracing joy.

5. Dwelling on the Past or Worrying about the Future: Many people spend too much time ruminating on past mistakes or worrying about future challenges. This prevents them from fully experiencing the present and finding happiness in the now. According to Eckhart Tolle in The Power of Now, true happiness comes from living in the present moment rather than dwelling on past regrets or future anxieties.

6. Lack of Self-Compassion: Individuals who are overly self-critical or lack self-compassion often find it difficult to experience happiness. They may feel they don't deserve happiness or they may be too focused on their flaws. Practicing self-compassion, as suggested by Kristin Neff, can help individuals be kinder to themselves and, in turn, feel more capable of experiencing joy.

True happiness comes from appreciating what you have, no matter how little. It comes from finding joy in the simplest of things—listening to a great song, a beautiful sunrise, the sound of laughter, a thoughtful phone call from a friend, or even the quiet gratitude of waking up pain-free.

One of the greatest lessons my mum taught me is to be content. Contentment does not mean giving up on your dreams or ambitions; it means being thankful for what you have now, even as you strive for greater things.

So, as you read this, I challenge you to pause and reflect: Are you happy? Are you finding joy in the life you're living today? Choose happiness—it's free. Learn to be grateful for where you are and what you have.

Because if you're miserable now in a small house, you'll be miserable in a mansion. If you're unhappy without a car, you'll soon find yourself unhappy in a luxury vehicle. Happiness begins in your heart, and no material thing can replace that. Find joy in the little things around you. When you learn to be content, everything else—cars, houses, promotions—becomes a bonus, not the source of your joy.

In summary, postponing happiness often stems from unrealistic expectations, seeking external approval, or avoiding emotions related to personal growth. Embracing a mindset of contentment with the present, letting go of perfectionism, and practicing self-compassion can help break these barriers to happiness.

Chapter two: Happiness is an inside job

I have come to understand that happiness is never something another person can give you,and its unfair to burden others with the responsibilities of making us happy. Happiness is not found in a husband, a boyfriend, or even in your children or friends. Happiness starts with you. Every morning when you wake up, you make a choice—to embrace joy or to let misery take root.

Happiness is an inside job. Yet, so many of us unconsciously place the weight of our happiness on the shoulders of others. This is especially true for women, who often tie their sense of worth and joy to how others treat them or fulfill their expectations.

In this book ,we highlight a powerful truth: no one else is responsible for your happiness. When we make others the source of our joy, we give away our power and set ourselves up for disappointment. Relationships thrive when they're built on love, respect, and partnership—not on the pressure to "make" someone happy.

For women, the key is learning to nurture happiness from within. This means investing in self-love, embracing your passions, and finding fulfillment in who you are, rather than relying on external validation. Your spouse, parents, or friends may enhance your life, but they are not the foundation of your joy.

Choosing happiness in relationships starts with letting go of unrealistic expectations and focusing on what you can control—your thoughts, actions, and attitude. When you take responsibility for your own happiness, you free others from an impossible burden and create space for healthier, more fulfilling connections.

When as women we place our happiness in our spouses, children, or friends, we unknowingly build our emotional foundation on shifting sands. When a spouse cheats, the betrayal can feel like a complete unraveling of our sense of self-worth and joy. If a child tragically passes away, the grief is compounded by the loss of the mothers sole source of fulfillment and purpose. When a close friend leaves or drifts apart, it can feel as though our happiness has been stolen. These devastating events expose the danger of outsourcing happiness—because when the person or relationship you've tied your joy to is no longer there, it can leave you feeling empty, broken, and lost. True peace and resilience come from within, not from others. Only by cultivating inner happiness can we navigate life's inevitable challenges without losing ourselves in the process.

"I would rather be single and happy than have a miserable marriage."That was my mantra during my late teenage years and early 20's.Growing up, all I ever seemed to hear was how miserable women were in their marriages. The women seemed so unhappy and moslty spoke of marriage as a chore and burden. And I kept wondering, if marriage is so bad, then why are people getting married at all?

I remember, years later, at my wedding, one of my mom's friends said something that shifted my perspective:

"All these women who keep complaining that marriage is hard, none of them have left. Marriage isn't as bad as they make it seem and what you make it."

I realized that there were women who were truly enjoying their marriages—women who radiated joy and fulfillment and I wanted to be one of them—and then there were others who seemed trapped in bitterness and misery. It dawned on me that the difference was not in the institution of marriage itself but in the choices people made within it.

From a young age, I resolved that if I ever got married, it would have to be to the right person, for the right reasons and I would be responsible for my own happiness. I began to observe the choices the women who were happy made and the mistakes I needed to avoid.

I had a pretty happy childhood and I wanted to continue being happy even in marriage,I remember praying and I asked God to let my marriage be an additional source of joy,love and growth, NOT my only source. Looking back now, I can say with gratitude that my prayer was answered. Has it been perfect? Of course not. Like every relationship, my marriage has had its ups and downs but very day I make decisions that ensure my peace and happiness.

This book is for every woman—whether you're single, married, or somewhere in between. It's about making the conscious choice to embrace joy, no matter your circumstances. It's about taking ownership of your happiness and understanding that it is not something you wait for or depend on others to provide.

Together, we'll explore how to build a life filled with peace, love, and fulfillment, regardless of your relationship status. Because happiness is not about having a perfect life or a perfect partner—it's about making the choice every day to live with joy and intention.

Chapter Three: The Power of Self-Talk

"I would rather be my own biggest supporter"

Every time I call my big sister, Carol, and ask her, "Hi, how are you?" She always responds with, "Blessed and highly favored." Imagine that—she calls herself blessed and highly favored, no matter what. Before she even mentions any challenges she might be facing, she's already declared her identity, her truth.

That response has always challenged me. Sometimes I catch myself replying with, "I'm not fine" Or "I'm just okay." Yet Carol, year after year, consistently speaks life over herself with those words: "Blessed and highly favored."

It's a powerful reminder to all of us—what are you calling yourself? Are you speaking negativity into your life, or are you affirming your blessings and your worth? The words you choose to describe yourself shape your mindset and your outlook. Choose words that empower, uplift, and remind you of who you truly are.

I have always been aware of the power of names, and my own story is a testament to this truth. When I was born, my father chose a name for me that carried a negative connotation—"Kamene," Which means "Hated" In our native tongue. My mother, however, purposed to give me the name 'mwende' "which translates to loved.

Looking back, I realize how profoundly being called "loved"

has shaped my life. I often wonder how different things might have been if I had carried the name my dad suggested "Unloved/hated." Words, especially names, carry immense power—they shape how we see ourselves and how others perceive us.

Many women unknowingly give themselves names, not necessarily spoken out loud but thought repeatedly in their minds: Ugly, fat, stupid, or unworthy. These labels become the lens through which they see themselves. What happens when a woman who has labeled herself "Ugly" Meets someone who calls her "Beautiful"? She anchors her happiness in that person's validation. If that person leaves, so does her happiness.

The words we speak to ourselves, consciously or subconsciously, have a profound impact on our emotional well-being and happiness. Self-talk—the inner dialogue we engage in daily—shapes how we perceive the world, respond to challenges, and ultimately determine our mental and emotional state. Positive self-talk can uplift and motivate us, while negative self-talk can lead to stress, self-doubt, and unhappiness.

A study conducted by Dr. Ethan Kross at the University of Michigan revealed the profound effects of self-talk on emotional regulation. In his research, participants who referred to themselves in the third person (e.g., "You can handle this" instead of "I can't handle this") were better able to distance themselves from negative emotions during stressful situations. This subtle change in perspective helped participants feel more in control and maintain a positive outlook, significantly reducing anxiety and increasing happiness.

Further studies have shown that consistent negative self-talk activates the brain's stress response, releasing cortisol, the hormone associated with stress. Chronic activation of this response can lead to feelings of sadness and even depression. Conversely, practicing positive affirmations—repeating uplifting statements to oneself—has been linked to increased activity in the brain's reward centers, releasing dopamine and creating feelings of joy and contentment.

In addition, a 2013 study published in the Journal of Personality and Social Psychology demonstrated that self-compassionate language—kind, forgiving words spoken internally—helps individuals cope with failures and setbacks more effectively. This approach not only reduces the intensity of negative emotions but also fosters resilience, a key component of happiness.

Transforming Self-Talk to Boost Happiness

The science is clear: the way we speak to ourselves directly influences our happiness and mental health. To harness this power, it's crucial to become aware of our inner dialogue and actively replace negative, critical thoughts with positive, affirming ones. For instance, instead of saying, "I always fail," one could say, "I'm learning and growing through this experience." Over time, this intentional shift can rewire the brain, creating a more optimistic mindset.

Happiness begins with the words we speak to ourselves. By choosing words of encouragement, self-compassion, and hope, we not only cultivate inner peace but also create a fertile ground for joy to flourish in every aspect of life.

So, I ask you: What are you calling yourself? Are you calling yourself beautiful, intelligent, and loved? Or are you labeling yourself with words that diminish your value?

Your source of happiness

One of the biggest mistakes we make is expecting happiness to come from external sources—whether it's a partner, a job, a child, or friendships. Let me be clear: If you weren't happy before you met someone, had that child, or got that job, you won't magically become happy because you received them.

Happiness is a choice. It's not a destination, and it doesn't depend on others. This is why we often hear women say they feel "Lost" When a relationship ends or a loved one is no longer there. While grief is natural, anchoring your entire sense of joy to another person or situation leaves you vulnerable.

Reclaiming your worth

Your worth does not come from your relationships, career, or external achievements. Your worth is intrinsic—it comes from the fact that you were created with a purpose. Whether you're married or single, a mother or not, employed or between jobs, you have value.

Society may pressure women to feel incomplete without a husband, children, or certain accomplishments. Fairy tales reinforce this myth, promising "Happily ever after" As soon as the heroine finds her prince. But let me tell you: You don't need a prince, a title, or any external marker to live a fulfilled, joyful life.

What name will you choose?

From this moment on, I challenge you to rename yourself with words that reflect the truth about your worth: Beautiful, loved, intelligent, valuable, purposeful. Choose names that affirm who you are and the life you want to live.

When you wake up each morning, decide to call yourself "Joyful." Remind yourself of your inherent value. Recognize that your happiness is in your hands, and no one else.

A final thought

You were created for a purpose. Whether or not you choose to have a partner, have children, or achieve societal milestones, you are enough. You are loved. You are valuable. And you were created to live a joyful life.

Chapter Four: Body image and happiness

How do you feel about yourself when you look in the mirror? For many of us, the answer is complicated. We focus on what we perceive as flaws, and in doing so, we deny ourselves the joy of celebrating the beautiful creation that we are.

I remember my struggles with body image. In primary school, I was the tallest girl in my class. I hated it. I hated towering over the boys, and I would think to myself, why do I have to be this tall? The idea troubled me so much that I dreamt of one day becoming rich enough to undergo surgery to reduce the length of my bones. Mind you, I had no idea such surgery even existed—it was just a desperate thought from a little girl who wanted to feel "Normal."

As I transitioned into adolescence, another insecurity emerged: My body began to change, and I became increasingly self-conscious. I remember being particularly uncomfortable when my breasts started growing bigger than those of my classmates.

These feelings, unfortunately, are not unique to me. So many women go through life feeling like their bodies are not enough—or too much. We compare ourselves to others, to impossible standards set by society, and we internalize the belief that we are not beautiful or worthy.

Improving body image is closely tied to fostering self-acceptance and cultivating practices that align with your mental and emotional well-being. Beyond positive self-talk, here are practical strategies to enhance how you perceive yourself inorder for you to live a happy life:

1. Focus on What Your Body Can Do

Shift the focus from appearance to functionality. Celebrate your body for its strength, resilience, and capabilities (e.g., walking, dancing, hugging loved ones).

Engage in physical activities you enjoy to appreciate movement and vitality.

2. Surround Yourself with Positivity

Follow social media accounts that promote body diversity and self-love rather than unrealistic standards.

Spend time with people who uplift and encourage you rather than those who focus on superficial traits.

3. Practice Gratitude

Write a list of things you are grateful for about your body and life in general. This helps redirect your thoughts toward appreciation.

4. Mindful Self-Care

Nurture your body with activities that make you feel good, like skincare routines, relaxing baths, wearing comfortable clothes, or getting enough sleep.

5. Avoid Comparisons

Remind yourself that everyone has unique features, and comparing yourself to others can diminish your self-worth. Focus on your personal journey.

6. Engage in Creative Expression

Participate in activities like painting, journaling, or dancing that allow you to express yourself freely and reconnect with your inner self.

7. Reframe Negative Thoughts

When a negative thought about your body arises, challenge it by finding a more compassionate perspective. For instance, instead of thinking, "I hate my arms," consider, "My arms help me hold the people I love."

8. Set Realistic Goals

If you want to work on aspects of your health or fitness, do so for your well-being rather than appearance. Focus on progress, not perfection.

9. Educate Yourself on Body Neutrality

Learn about body neutrality, which focuses on accepting your body without necessarily loving or hating it. This perspective promotes peace with your appearance.

10. Therapy and Support Groups

Consider therapy or support groups to address deeper issues related to self-esteem and body image. Professionals can help reframe limiting beliefs and build self-acceptance.

11. Invest in Personal Style

Wear clothes that make you feel confident and comfortable. Experiment with styles that celebrate your personality and make you feel good.

12. Practice Daily Affirmations

Start your day by affirming your worth and capabilities. Statements like, "I am enough just as I am," can set a positive tone.

By combining these practices with positive self-talk, you can build a healthier relationship with your body and enhance your happiness. What resonates with you the most from these suggestions?

The toll of negative self-talk

When we are unkind to ourselves, it shows. Negative self-talk chips away at our self-esteem. We look at our reflection and focus on everything we dislike, reinforcing a cycle of dissatisfaction and unhappiness.

Imagine this: You tell yourself daily that you're not beautiful, that you're too fat, too thin, too dark, or too tall. Over time, these words shape your perception of yourself. Then, one day, someone comes along and tells you you're beautiful. For a moment, you feel uplifted. But if that person's validation is the only thing holding up your self-worth, what happens when they leave?

This is why it's essential to change the narrative.

Rewriting your story

Your body is not a mistake. It's not a problem to be fixed or a project to be perfected. Your body is a gift—a vessel that allows you to experience life. The moment you start embracing it as it is, you'll unlock a new level of joy and freedom.

I wish I could go back and tell my younger self that being tall was not a curse, but a unique feature that made me stand out. I wish I could tell her that her height was something to be proud of, not something to hide. But since I can't rewrite the past, I have made it my mission to speak this truth to others now:

Your beauty is not defined by anyone else's opinion or by societal standards. Your beauty is inherent, and it's yours to own. Growing up you could hardly see a black person on the runway only the ladies who had light skin were considered beautiful, but now that has changed we see the likes of beautiful Khoudia Diop defying the beauty standards we had growing up in the 80s and 90s.

There's an undeniable link between how we perceive our bodies and how happy we feel. When we stop fighting against our bodies and start accepting them, we free ourselves from the constant pressure to conform.

Acceptance doesn't mean you can't work towards being healthier or stronger; it means you do so out of love for your body, not because you hate it.

The next time you look in the mirror, I challenge you to replace criticism with kindness. Instead of saying, "I hate my thighs," Say, "These legs carry me every day." Instead of thinking, "I wish I looked like her," Remind yourself, "I am uniquely me, and that's enough."

Your journey to happiness starts with self-love. By embracing your body as it is, you permit yourself to experience the fullness of life without the weight of self-doubt.

Psalm 139:14NIV

> I praise you because I am fearfully and wonderfully made;
> your works are wonderful,
> I know that full well.

Chapter Five: Enjoy your own company

“I would rather enjoy my own company than feel miserable in the midst of a crowd”

Many people struggle with spending time alone, but the challenges vary depending on personality and character traits. Extroverts, for example, often thrive on social interaction and may feel restless or lonely when they're by themselves. They might struggle to fill the quiet moments, interpreting solitude as boredom or isolation. Introverts, on the other hand, may initially relish alone time but can fall into overthinking or dwelling on negative thoughts if they don't consciously engage in uplifting activities.

To overcome these struggles, it's important to shift the mindset from "being alone" to "spending quality time with yourself." Start by exploring activities that bring joy and personal growth. For instance, an extrovert might enjoy dancing or singing to their favorite playlist, creating energy and positivity even without a crowd. An introvert could delve into reading a book or journaling, allowing them to reflect in a structured way that prevents overthinking. Both personality types could benefit from activities like cooking a delicious meal, taking a walk in nature, or watching a favorite movie—each offering moments of creativity, relaxation, and self-care.

The key is to focus on what makes you feel happy and fulfilled. By treating alone time as an opportunity for self-discovery and enjoyment, you can learn to appreciate your own company and build a deeper connection with yourself.

Additionally, enjoying your own company can extend to activities like taking solo road trips, treating yourself to a nice meal at a restaurant, or savoring a peaceful moment with a cup of coffee at your favorite café. It's empowering to realize that you don't always need to be in the presence of others to enjoy life. Learning to love your own company means embracing the freedom to pursue the things that make you happy, without waiting for someone else to join you.

For the longest time, I hesitated to do things alone. The idea of going to a spa or even stepping out for a solo meal felt strange, almost as if I needed permission to enjoy myself. But now, I've learned to appreciate these moments. Taking yourself out is not just about the activity itself—it's about acknowledging your worth and treating yourself as someone deserving of care and joy. When you stop limiting yourself by waiting for company, you open the door to richer experiences and deeper self-connection. It's liberating to know you can create happiness on your terms.

Many of us are constantly seeking validation from others, believing that our happiness depends on being surrounded by the right people, or in the case of women, having the right relationship. But the truth is, the greatest form of happiness and contentment comes from within. The ability to enjoy your own company is an invaluable skill, one that allows you to be at peace no matter your external circumstances.

The power of solitude

Learning to enjoy your own company is not about being isolated or lonely; rather, it is about appreciating your own presence, embracing your solitude, and finding joy in your own thoughts, actions, and reflections. Solitude is not an enemy—it's a space where you can connect with yourself on a deeper level. This connection with yourself is where true self-love and happiness begin.

When we can stand alone without feeling incomplete, we empower ourselves. No longer do we need to rely on others to feel validated. Our self-worth becomes intrinsic. We realize that we are whole, regardless of our relationship status, social circle, or career.

Creating a fulfilling solo life

To truly enjoy your own company, it's essential to engage in activities that bring you joy, peace, and fulfillment—without needing someone else to validate them. This could mean pursuing hobbies that make you feel alive, learning new skills, or simply spending quiet time reflecting. Reading, cooking, painting, walking in nature, and even taking yourself out to a nice restaurant are all great ways to fill your cup.

When we invest in our growth, happiness, and self-care, we send a message to ourselves: "I am enough." Over time, we begin to understand that our happiness is not dependent on others. It's a choice we make every day.

Embrace self-discovery

Spending time with yourself is a perfect opportunity for self-discovery. It's a chance to listen to your inner voice and explore your desires, fears, and passions. Many of us get so caught up in the demands of relationships or societal expectations that we forget to check in with ourselves. Who are you when no one is around? What do you truly enjoy? What dreams are you too afraid to pursue?

This chapter encourages you to take time for self-reflection. Maybe you've been so focused on what others think or have been trying to fit into someone else's mold that you've forgotten what truly makes you happy. By enjoying your own company, you start to rediscover the unique, amazing person you are—and the limitless potential you have.

The joy of being alone, not lonely

There is a significant difference between being alone and feeling lonely. Loneliness arises from feeling disconnected, often due to a perceived lack of external validation or connection. On the other hand, being alone is a conscious choice, a space for peace and rejuvenation.

When we enjoy our own company, we no longer fear being alone. Instead, we see it as an opportunity to grow, recharge, and center ourselves. Loneliness, which once felt like a void, transforms into a space for personal growth and reflection.

The key to healthy relationships

One of the most beautiful things about enjoying your own company is that it prepares you for healthier, more balanced relationships with others. When you are whole and content with yourself, you are less likely to place unrealistic expectations on others to make you happy. Instead, you attract people who share similar values and who are also content with themselves. You don't need them to complete you; you are already complete.

If you're not comfortable with yourself, you'll always be searching for someone to fill that void. But when you find joy in your own company, you approach relationships with an open heart and a healthy perspective. You can love someone else without needing them to validate your self-worth.

Conclusion

Ultimately, enjoying your own company is about recognizing your inherent value and making yourself a priority. It's a mindset shift—one that acknowledges you are complete on your own, that your happiness is not determined by external factors or the presence of others, and that solitude is an opportunity to reconnect with your true self. When you learn to enjoy your own company, you unlock the potential to live a more fulfilled, joyful, and empowered life.

In the end, remember: You are enough, just as you are. And the best relationship you will ever have is the one you have with yourself.

Chapter Six: Surround yourself with people who value you

"I would rather have one good friend than ten who are fake "

Once you've mastered the art of enjoying your own company, the next step is to surround yourself with people who uplift, value, and inspire you. As much as solitude is essential for self-reflection and growth, human beings are inherently social. We thrive in relationships where we feel seen, heard, and appreciated. The company we keep plays a significant role in shaping who we are and how we view ourselves.

The people you surround yourself with play a crucial role in your happiness. They can either uplift and inspire you or drain your energy and contribute to your unhappiness. For the longest time, I struggled with setting boundaries, especially at work. I found it hard to say no, particularly to my bosses, who, noticing my efficiency, would keep piling work on me while my colleagues relaxed. This left me overwhelmed and unhappy. Over time, I realized that boundaries are essential for protecting my happiness, not just at work but also in friendships and other relationships.

To set boundaries at work, start by clearly defining your limits. If your workload is unmanageable, have an honest conversation with your boss, explaining the impact on your productivity and well-being. Politely but firmly say, "I'd love to help, but I'm currently at capacity. Can the work wait or can we redistribute tasks?" Similarly, in friendships, communicate openly when you feel taken for granted. If someone constantly demands your time without reciprocating, it's okay to say, "I value our friendship, but I need to focus on some personal things right now."

Remember, boundaries are not about shutting people out; they're about preserving your energy and happiness. Enforcing boundaries may feel uncomfortable initially, especially if you're a people-pleaser like I was, but it's an act of self-respect. When you set clear boundaries, you teach others how to treat you and create space for more balanced, fulfilling relationships. In doing so, you safeguard your happiness and maintain a sense of control over your life.

The importance of meaningful connections

Having people in your life who genuinely see your worth can be transformative. They encourage you, challenge you, and remind you of your potential, especially during moments of doubt. True friends celebrate your wins and hold space for you in your losses. They push you to grow, and, most importantly, they remind you of your inherent value when you forget it yourself.

For me, one such person has been my best friend, Irene. We met in high school, and though I am naturally introverted and often content in my own space, Irene saw something in me that I didn't see in myself. Over the years, she consistently encouraged me to step out of my comfort zone—to attend meetings, connect with other women, and embrace new experiences. Her unwavering support and belief in me made me realize how powerful it is to have someone in your corner who values you.

Identifying your support system

Not everyone deserves a seat at your table. Surrounding yourself with people who value you requires discernment. Here are some questions to help you identify the right people to keep close:

Do they encourage your growth? True friends and loved ones push you toward becoming the best version of yourself. They don't hold you back or make you feel small.

Do they celebrate your successes? People who value you will genuinely rejoice in your achievements, no matter how big or small.

Do they respect your boundaries? Healthy relationships are built on mutual respect. People who truly value you will honor your limits without question.

Do they bring positivity into your life? While no relationship is perfect, the people you surround yourself with should bring more light than darkness into your life.

The power of letting go

It's equally important to let go of relationships that drain you or make you feel less than you are. Not everyone is meant to stay in your life forever, and that's okay. Sometimes, letting go of toxic or one-sided relationships creates space for healthier, more fulfilling connections to blossom.

This doesn't mean cutting people off without reason, but rather being intentional about who you allow into your inner circle. You deserve to be surrounded by people who see your value and treat you accordingly.

Building a tribe that aligns with your values

Your tribe doesn't have to be large—it just needs to consist of people who align with your values and bring out the best in you. These individuals might include:

Friends: Friends who see your potential and encourage you to reach it are invaluable.

Family: Not all family relationships are positive, but when you have family members who uplift and support you, they can form a strong foundation for your personal growth.

Mentors: Seek out mentors who inspire and guide you, offering wisdom and perspective.

Community: Whether it's a church group, a professional network, or a hobby club, communities that share your interests and values can provide a sense of belonging.

Reciprocate the value

While it's essential to surround yourself with people who value you, it's equally important to offer the same in return. Be the kind of friend, partner, or family member who lifts others, celebrates their victories, and supports them in their struggles. Relationships thrive when they're built on mutual respect, love, and encouragement.

Conclusion

The people you surround yourself with have the power to shape your mindset, influence your decisions, and impact your overall happiness. Choose wisely. Seek out those who see your worth, celebrate your successes, and encourage your growth. Just as importantly, be intentional about letting go of relationships that no longer serve you.

Remember, you are deserving of love, respect, and support. The right people will remind you of that truth every day, just as you will remind them. As you nurture these meaningful relationships, you'll find that your life becomes richer, more fulfilling, and beautifully balanced.

Proverbs 27:17

New English Translation

As iron sharpens iron,
so a person sharpens his friend.

Chapter Seven: "I would rather have a happy marriage"

Most marriages today are unhappy because one partner insists on winning every argument, constantly trying to prove they are right. While being right might feel satisfying in the moment, it's important to recognize that happiness in a relationship often comes from mutual respect, understanding, and compromise. Being right doesn't mean you need to force your perspective onto your spouse or push it down their throat. True happiness comes when both partners feel heard and valued, even in disagreements. It's not about proving a point but about fostering harmony and connection. Sometimes, letting go of the need to 'win' an argument can preserve peace and strengthen the bond between partners.

Another threat to happiness in marriage lies in the friends we surround ourselves with. The wrong kind of influence—be it unwise counsel, constant venting, or advice from someone who doesn't understand the dynamics of a committed relationship—can cause more harm than good. I've seen married individuals take advice from their single friends, and destroyed their marriages not realizing the vast difference in their circumstances. Marriage requires compromise, wisdom, and the ability to navigate challenges within the unique framework of your relationship.

When faced with marital difficulties, it's tempting to call a friend for guidance. While this can be helpful, it's vital to ensure that your confidants are wise, grounded, and invested in your relationship's success.

Poor advice can sow seeds of discord and, in extreme cases, jeopardize your relationship entirely.

Marriage is about finding balance. It's learning to compromise without sacrificing your happiness. True happiness in marriage doesn't depend on circumstances; it's an intentional choice. My favorite analogy is this: the moment my husband walks through the door, I ask myself, What do I want for this moment? Do I want happiness, peace, or conflict? For me, the choice is clear—I choose happiness.

This simple yet profound decision can transform your marriage. By setting the tone for peace and joy, you create an atmosphere where love can flourish, even amid disagreements. After all, the greatest gift you can give your relationship is the conscious decision to foster harmony and happiness, both for yourself and your partner.

Marriage is a beautiful union, but it requires conscious effort from both partners to thrive. As wives, we often carry the weight of setting the tone for the home, especially in terms of emotional atmosphere. The environment we cultivate within our marriage and home plays a significant role in shaping the happiness of everyone in the household. The saying, "If mama isn't happy, even the cats are sad," May sound humorous, but it holds a truth: A wife's mood can have a ripple effect on the entire family.

In this chapter, we explore how wives can make the daily choice to be happy, choose their battles wisely, and intentionally create a peaceful environment that fosters joy and fulfillment in marriage.

Choose your battles: Let go of what doesn't matter.

Marriage is full of moments where conflict could arise, but not every disagreement needs to turn into a battle. One of the most important decisions a wife can make is choosing which battles are worth fighting for. Not every issue or mistake needs to be addressed immediately, and not everything requires a confrontation. Sometimes, letting go of small annoyances can save your energy and preserve the peace that you value so much.

In every relationship, disagreements are inevitable. However, the way we deal with these issues plays a critical role in determining the health of that relationship—whether it's a marriage, friendship, or familial bond. The key lies in understanding the how, when, and where of addressing conflicts. These three pillars are pivotal in maintaining harmony and fostering happiness.

How

"A soft answer turns away wrath, but a harsh word stirs up anger" (Proverbs 15:1). The tone and words you choose when addressing an issue can either escalate or diffuse tension. Speaking gently, even in the face of frustration, can transform a heated argument into a constructive conversation. Sometimes, simply saying, "I'm sorry," even when you feel you're not at fault, can help quell discord and pave the way for resolution. Humility and grace often carry more weight than proving a point.

When

Timing is everything. Not every issue requires immediate resolution. Ask yourself, Does this have to be dealt with now? Sometimes, giving it a moment or waiting until tempers have cooled can make all the difference. A calmer mind leads to clearer communication and a greater chance of finding common ground.

Where

The environment in which you address conflicts matters too. Consider discussing sensitive matters in neutral, calming spaces—over a cup of coffee, on an evening walk, or away from the stressors of home. A change of scenery can shift the dynamic of the conversation, making it easier to focus on resolution rather than escalation.

When choosing your battles, remember this: not every fight is worth the cost of your peace. By being intentional about how, when, and where you address conflicts, you can uphold happiness and nurture the love that binds your relationship. Ultimately, choosing happiness sometimes means choosing harmony over being right.

Ephesians 4:2-3 reminds us:

"Be completely humble and gentle; be patient, bearing with one another in love. Make every effort to keep the unity of the spirit through the bond of peace."

Choosing your battles is not about avoiding confrontation but about discerning which issues truly matter and which ones can be forgiven or overlooked. When you choose peace over petty disagreements, you allow the relationship to grow in a healthy way, and your home remains an environment where love and joy flourish.

Decide what kind of marriage you want.

Every marriage is unique, and as wives, we must decide what kind of marriage we want to build. Do we want a marriage filled with constant tension, frustration, and misunderstandings? Or do we want one of mutual respect, joy, and growth? The choice is ours.

By making a conscious decision to nurture our marriages with love, respect, and communication, we set the stage for a thriving relationship. Marriage isn't just about living together—it's about creating a partnership that encourages both individuals to grow spiritually, emotionally, and mentally.

Proverbs 24:3-4 says:

"By wisdom, a house is built, and through understanding, it is established; through knowledge, its rooms are filled with rare and beautiful treasures."

A healthy marriage is built on wisdom, understanding, and knowledge. It requires intentional decisions about how we communicate, love, and support our spouses. When we choose to prioritize these things, we create an environment where both partners can experience true happiness and fulfillment.

Women are the mood-setters in the home.

In any relationship, especially in marriage, mood plays a significant role in shaping the overall atmosphere of the home. As wives, we often hold the power to influence the emotional climate of the household. Our reactions, behaviors, and attitudes can either bring peace and joy or create tension and frustration.

Proverbs 14:1 highlights this:

"The wise woman builds her house, but with her own hands, the foolish one tears hers down."

A wise woman knows that the energy she brings to the home will set the tone for the day. Whether we recognize it or not, our emotions affect those around us—our spouses, children, and even extended family. As wives, we have the responsibility to create an environment that promotes peace, love, and happiness.

When we choose to respond with patience, kindness, and understanding, even in challenging moments, we create a nurturing and supportive atmosphere. This doesn't mean avoiding conflict but rather addressing it in a way that upholds respect and love.

What kind of environment do you want in your house?

The atmosphere of your home reflects your values, priorities, and the love you have for your family. Think about the environment you want to create: Is it one filled with peace, love, and laughter? Or is it tense and filled with unspoken frustrations?

I deeply value peace. Without peace, happiness is impossible. Peace allows us to think clearly, communicate effectively, and make decisions with love and wisdom. In a peaceful environment, the whole family can thrive.

Colossians 3:15 encourages us:

"Let the peace of Christ rule in your hearts, since as members of one body you were called to peace. And be thankful."

Peace is not just the absence of conflict; it is the presence of Christ in our hearts, ruling over our emotions, actions, and relationships. When we prioritize peace, we create a foundation for happiness that allows everyone in the home to feel safe, valued, and loved.

The power of intentional joy

Happiness in marriage doesn't just happen; it is a choice. Every day, we can choose to focus on the positives, appreciate our spouses, and be grateful for the small joys that come with being together. Joy is a decision, and it's one we can make each day, even when life is busy or difficult.

Psalm 118:24 reminds us:

"This is the day the lord has made; let us rejoice and be glad in it."

Even when things aren't perfect, we can choose joy in the day that god has given us. This joy stems from knowing that our happiness is not dependent on our circumstances but on the presence of god in our lives and in our marriages. When we choose to rejoice and be glad in the day, we open the door to lasting happiness in our relationships.

Peace is the key to happiness in marriage.

At the heart of a joyful marriage is peace. Without peace, there is no room for happiness. When we prioritize peace, we create a space for love, respect, and happiness to grow. Peace doesn't mean that there won't be challenges or disagreements, but it means that we will handle them in a way that promotes healing, understanding, and unity.

To have a happy marriage, we must choose daily to cultivate peace, choose our battles wisely, and create an environment where love, respect, and joy can flourish. When we do this, we not only experience happiness in our hearts but also create a home where everyone feels valued, supported, and loved.

Conclusion: The daily choice of happiness

In marriage, happiness is not something that just happens—it is something that must be chosen daily. As wives, we have the power to influence the emotional climate of our homes, and by choosing peace, joy, and love, we can create a marriage that is fulfilling and joyful. Let us choose wisely the kind of marriage we want, let go of the small battles that don't matter, and set the tone for peace and happiness in our homes.

Chapter Eight: Giving

One of the most profound experiences in my life came when I was introduced to New Life Children's Home by Irene my best friend since high school, she showed me the joy of giving when she took me to visit this children's home, and even now she consistently encourages our group of women to support those in need. The home cared for newborns and babies up to I think the age of two, and every time we visited, we spent the afternoon feeding, playing, and holding the babies. It was a simple act, but the joy it brought me was beyond words.

I remember holding a newborn in my arms, looking at their tiny fingers and their beautiful toothless smiles. Their joy, despite their circumstances, was contagious. It was as if the babies knew that they were loved and cared for, even for just a few hours, and that love spread through the entire room.

Seeing their smiles, hearing their laughter, and witnessing their trust in us to care for them—it all gave me a deep sense of fulfillment. The pure happiness they felt just from us being there to love them was something I could never have imagined. In those moments, I realized that life is not just about what we have or what we accomplish, but how we share what we have with others.

Living life to the fullest is about more than just seeking personal happiness—it's about embracing the joy that comes from serving others and making a positive impact in the world around you. True fulfillment often arises from what we give to others, whether it's our time, resources, or love. When we dedicate ourselves to helping others, we not only enhance their lives but also deepen our sense of purpose and joy.

The relationship between giving and happiness is profound and well-documented, both spiritually and scientifically. Here's how they connect:

1. Spiritual Perspective

Biblical Principles: The Bible teaches that giving leads to blessings and joy. For instance, "It is more blessed to give than to receive" (Acts 20:35). Generosity reflects God's nature and aligns us with His purpose, bringing inner peace and fulfillment.

Sense of Purpose: Giving allows you to make a difference in others' lives, which can strengthen your faith and deepen your connection with God and people.

2. Emotional and Psychological Benefits

Joy and Gratitude: When you give, you feel joy in knowing you've helped someone. This act often shifts your focus from scarcity to abundance, increasing gratitude for what you have.

Reduced Stress: Giving activates the brain's reward system, releasing "feel-good" hormones like dopamine, serotonin, and oxytocin, which reduce stress and enhance overall happiness.

Sense of Connection: Acts of giving foster relationships and strengthen bonds, combating feelings of loneliness or isolation.

3. Practical and Everyday Impacts

Shift from Self-Centeredness: Focusing on others through giving helps break cycles of self-centered thinking, which is often linked to dissatisfaction or unhappiness.

Pay-it-Forward Effect: Your generosity inspires others to give, creating a ripple effect of positivity that enhances community well-being and spreads joy.

4. Science of Giving and Happiness

Studies on Altruism: Research consistently shows that people who give—whether time, money, or resources—report higher levels of life satisfaction. For example:

A 2008 Harvard study found that spending money on others boosts happiness more than spending it on oneself.

Volunteering has been linked to lower rates of depression and longer life expectancy.

Reciprocity Effect: Giving often leads to receiving in unexpected ways, such as support, opportunities, or emotional rewards.

5. Types of Giving That Enhance Happiness

Financial Giving: Supporting causes or helping someone in need gives a sense of empowerment and gratitude.

Time and Effort: Volunteering or mentoring allows you to see the immediate impact of your contributions.

Acts of Kindness: Small, everyday acts like sharing a smile or helping someone in need can create moments of joy.

Giving is a powerful pathway to happiness because it aligns us with higher purposes, strengthens our connections, and shifts focus from what we lack to how we can bless others. When you give with a sincere heart, you not only bring joy to others but also cultivate lasting happiness within yourself.

The joy of serving others

I have found that the more I serve others, the more joy fills my heart. It is in giving that we truly receive. Serving others allows us to step outside of our own needs and focus on making someone else's life a little brighter. Whether it's through acts of kindness, volunteering our time, or offering a helping hand, the impact is immeasurable.

The power of kindness

Kindness is a powerful tool that can transform lives. A simple act of kindness, whether it's a smile, a helping hand, or a thoughtful gesture, can make a world of difference to someone who is struggling. When we treat others with kindness, we not only uplift their spirits but also enrich our own lives. Acts of kindness have a ripple effect—they spread joy not only to the person receiving the kindness but also to everyone who witnesses it.

Jesus reminds us in Matthew 25:40:

"Truly I tell you, whatever you did for one of the least of these brothers and sisters of mine, you did for me."

When we show kindness, we are, in essence, showing love to god through his people. It's a reminder that our acts of service are not just for the benefit of others—they are a way of serving god and reflecting his love in the world.

Giving of your time and resources

True fulfillment comes from giving. When we give of our time, talents, and resources, we open ourselves to the fullness of life. Whether it's donating our time to a cause, sharing our resources with those in need, or offering our skills to help others, giving enriches both the giver and the receiver.

I learned this lesson early on in life, especially during my visits to the children's home. What we gave—our time and love—may have seemed small in the grand scheme of things, but the joy and peace it brought were immeasurable. It was in those simple acts of service that I felt the most connected to my purpose, and it was through those moments that I truly learned the importance of giving.

As we grow older and gain more in life, it becomes easier to forget the value of giving. We may become caught up in the pursuit of material possessions or personal success, but true happiness doesn't come from what we acquire—it comes from what we give away. Proverbs 11:25 teaches us:

"A generous person will prosper; whoever refreshes others will be refreshed."

The more we give, the more we receive in return—not just in material wealth, but in joy, love, and spiritual fulfillment. Giving opens our hearts to the world around us and fills our lives with purpose.

Living with purpose

Living life to the fullest means living with purpose. It's not just about seeking happiness for ourselves, but about finding meaning in how we serve others. Each act of kindness, no matter how small, has the potential to change the world. When we live with the mindset of giving, we can make a lasting impact, not just in the lives of those we serve, but in our hearts as well.

Philippians 2:4 encourages us to:

"Let each of you look not only to his interests but also to the interests of others."

When we focus on the needs of others, we fulfill a deeper sense of purpose. Serving others not only helps them but also brings us closer to our true calling. Life is about connection, and through service, we form meaningful bonds that enrich our lives and the lives of those around us.

The lasting joy of giving fully

The more I have served others, the more I have experienced the deep joy that comes from knowing that my life is making a difference. I've learned that living life to the fullest is not about achieving fame or fortune, but about using what we have to make the world a better place. The joy I felt feeding those babies at the children's home still lingers in my heart, reminding me that the most meaningful experiences in life come not from what we get, but from what we give.

In every moment of kindness, in every act of service, we find a piece of our purpose. And as we give, we also receive. This is the fullness of life: To live with love, purpose, and joy, sharing what we have and lifting up those around us. It's not about living for ourselves—it's about living for others, and in doing so, we find our greatest joy.

Chapter Nine: Love unconditionally

"I would rather love than hate"

We all want to be loved whether it's by our parents, siblings, or even friends, love is one of the most powerful forces in the world. It transcends boundaries, heals wounds, and connects people in ways that nothing else can. God loves you unconditionally, and as his creation, he calls us to love others in the same way. Love is not just an emotion—it's a decision, an intentional choice to care for and uplift those around us, regardless of their flaws or shortcomings.

Love and Happiness: A Scientific Perspective

The profound connection between love and happiness has been a topic of fascination for researchers for decades. One of the most compelling studies on this relationship is the Harvard Study of Adult Development, which began in 1938 and continues to this day. This study tracked the lives of 724 men over several decades to understand what contributes to a fulfilling life.

The findings were remarkable: the quality of relationships—not wealth, fame, or career success—was the strongest predictor of happiness and overall well-being. Participants who reported having strong, supportive connections (romantic, familial, or platonic) were consistently happier, healthier, and even lived longer than those who were socially isolated.

One of the study's directors, Dr. Robert Waldinger, summarized it succinctly: "Good relationships keep us happier and healthier. Period." It wasn't just about having relationships but the quality of those connections. Love in all its forms—romantic, familial, platonic, or even self-love—served as a protective factor against stress, depression, and loneliness.

This research aligns with the idea that love fosters a sense of belonging, emotional security, and purpose, which are foundational to happiness. Whether it's the love of a spouse, the bond between friends, or the unconditional affection from family, these relationships are central to our emotional and psychological well-being.

I would rather than love than hate because, living in hate profoundly affects a person's well-being, spirit, and capacity for joy. Here's how:

1. Mental and Emotional Health

Chronic Stress: Hatred often fuels a constant state of negativity and tension, leading to elevated stress levels. This can trigger anxiety, depression, and mood swings.

Negative Thought Patterns: It fosters a cycle of bitterness, resentment, and anger, which consumes mental energy and diminishes emotional resilience.

Isolation: Hate can push others away, leaving the individual lonely and disconnected, which exacerbates feelings of unhappiness.

2. Physical Health

Impact on the Heart: Prolonged anger and hatred can lead to increased blood pressure, heart disease, and other stress-related illnesses.

Weakened Immune System: The body's stress response can suppress immunity, making it harder to fight off infections and recover from illnesses.

Sleep Disorders: Hatred often disrupts peace of mind, leading to poor sleep quality or insomnia, which further affects physical health.

3. Spiritual Well-being

Disconnection from Peace: Hate creates an inner turmoil that blocks feelings of peace, gratitude, and spiritual fulfillment.

Barrier to Growth: It hinders forgiveness, love, and compassion, which are essential for spiritual maturity and a deeper connection with God or one's higher purpose.

Loss of Purpose: Living in hate distracts from meaningful pursuits, leaving one spiritually stagnant and unfulfilled.

4. Joy and Fulfillment

Erodes Joy: Hate overshadows positive experiences, making it difficult to find happiness in life's blessings.

Blocks Relationships: Genuine joy often comes from meaningful connections with others, which hatred disrupts.

Stifles Gratitude: It focuses attention on negatives, preventing the individual from appreciating life's beauty and goodness.

Transforming Hate to Healing

Choosing forgiveness, understanding, and love can reverse these effects. It renews the mind, restores physical health, and reignites spiritual and emotional joy. As the Bible teaches, love and forgiveness bring freedom and healing, while hate binds the heart in chains. Letting go of hate is essential to living a life of peace and fulfillment.

Our ability to love others often starts with our ability to accept and love ourselves. Here are some thoughts and practical steps to help you embrace love more fully and extend it to others:

1. Recognize Your Worth

Understand that you are inherently valuable and deserving of love, not because of what you do but simply because of who you are.

Reflect on scriptures or affirmations that remind you of this truth, such as "I am fearfully and wonderfully made" (Psalm 139:14).

2. Address Past Hurts

Unresolved pain can make it hard to accept love. Seek healing through counseling, prayer, or conversations with trusted individuals who can help you process past wounds.

Forgive yourself and others—it clears the way to receive and give love.

3. Practice Self-Compassion

Speak kindly to yourself. Replace self-criticism with encouragement.

Treat yourself with the same patience and understanding you'd offer to a friend.

4. Allow Others to Love You

Let people care for you without feeling guilty or unworthy. Accept compliments, help, and affection without deflecting them.

Start small: say "thank you" when someone expresses kindness instead of brushing it off.

5. Engage in Acts of Love

Practice loving others even when you don't feel like it—actions often shape feelings. Simple acts of kindness build the habit of unconditional love.

Notice how giving love enriches your happiness and deepens connections.

6. Strengthen Your Relationship with God

God's love is the purest and most unconditional. Spend time in prayer, worship, and studying His Word to experience His love deeply.

Ask Him to fill your heart with His love so that it overflows to others.

7. Be Present in Relationships

Listen actively and empathize with others. Building trust and connection helps both you and the other person feel valued.

Love often grows when we focus on others instead of our insecurities.

I remember when my children were young, they loved my cakes now and I equally enjoyed baking with each of them ready and willing to help. The simple act of preparing something with love, and then watching them enjoy it, brought me such immense happiness. My happiness was in the experience of serving my family, seeing their joy, and knowing that I had created something that brought warmth into our home.

Acknowledge when you've allowed love in—whether it's a smile, a hug, or a kind word.

Reflect on moments when you gave love and felt joy from it.

The power of unconditional love

Unconditional love is a reflection of god's love for us. His love is not based on our actions, behaviors, or worthiness—it's given freely, without conditions. In the same way, we are called to love others without expecting anything in return. When we love others unconditionally, we mirror god's love and create an atmosphere of peace, joy, and connection.

In John 15:12, Jesus commands us to:

"My command is this: Love each other as I have loved you."

This love is not limited by circumstances or emotions—it is a decision to choose love, no matter what. Just as god's love for us never wavers, our love for others should be constant, no matter their flaws, mistakes, or imperfections.

Purposefully loving those around you.

I have made it a point in my life to ensure that everyone I love knows how i feel about them. Whether it's family, friends, or those I care for, I want them to feel valued, cherished, and supported. Love is not something we should keep hidden in our hearts—it's something we should express and share with others. It's through our words, actions, and presence that we demonstrate love to those around us.

This purposeful expression of love has brought me an incredible sense of fulfillment. The more love I give, the more love I receive in return. There's a beauty in the reciprocal nature of love—it's like a cycle that continually flows, nurturing and growing each person it touches.

When we give love freely, we open ourselves to receiving love in return, which enriches our lives in ways we cannot measure.

Luke 6:38 tells us:

"Give, and it will be given to you. A good measure, pressed down, shaken together, and running over, will be poured into your lap. For with the measure you use, it will be measured to you."

The more we give, the more we receive. This principle applies not only to material things but also to love, kindness, and compassion. When we love others unconditionally, we invite love to flow back into our lives in abundance.

Love and healing

Love is a healing force. When we offer love to others, it has the power to heal emotional wounds, mend broken relationships, and restore peace in our hearts. Loving unconditionally allows us to let go of grudges, resentment, and bitterness. It helps us see beyond a person's mistakes and flaws, allowing us to embrace them as they are.

In my own life, I have experienced the healing power of unconditional love. When I choose to love others, even when it's difficult, I find that it brings peace to my heart and strengthens my relationships. It's through love that we build trust, understanding, and connection. Love is the foundation of all strong relationships, and when we love without conditions, we create a safe and nurturing space for growth and healing.

God's love as the model

God's love is our ultimate model. He loved us while we were still sinners, and he continues to love us, even when we fall short of his standards. This is the kind of love we are called to extend to others. Romans 5:8 says:

"But god demonstrates his love toward us, in that while we were still sinners, Christ died for us."

God's love is unconditional, sacrificial, and unwavering. He did not wait for us to be perfect before he loved us—he loved us first. This is the kind of love we should aim to reflect in our relationships with others.

Living a life of unconditional love

Choosing to love unconditionally is not always easy. There will be times when people hurt us, disappoint us, or frustrate us. But the key to unconditional love is understanding that it is not based on the other person's actions but on our decision to love. When we choose to love, even in difficult situations, we align ourselves with god's will and reflect his love to the world.

Love is a journey. The more you practice receiving and giving it, the more natural it becomes, leading to greater happiness and deeper relationships.

Chapter Ten: Find Your Purpose

One of the greatest sources of joy in my life is knowing that at the end of each day, I have accomplished something meaningful. There's something incredibly fulfilling about setting a goal and working toward it, knowing that at the end of the day, you've made progress. Purpose is the driving force that propels us to live a life full of meaning and satisfaction.

The power of purpose

The power of purpose is profound when it comes to happiness and living a healthy, fulfilling life. Here's an exploration of why purpose matters and how it contributes to health and well-being:

1. Purpose as a Source of Happiness

Meaning Beyond Self: When you live a purpose-driven life, you align your actions with values and goals that resonate deeply within you. This alignment generates a sense of fulfillment and joy that goes beyond fleeting pleasures.

Intrinsic Motivation: Purpose fuels intrinsic motivation, where you feel driven by passion and meaning rather than external rewards. This creates sustained happiness that isn't dependent on circumstances.

2. Purpose and Emotional Well-being

Resilience in Adversity: People with a clear sense of purpose are better equipped to handle challenges. Purpose acts as an anchor, providing clarity and stability even during tough times.

Reduced Stress and Anxiety: When you focus on serving your purpose, you experience less inner turmoil. Your energy is channeled into meaningful activities, leaving little room for worry and self-doubt.

3. Purpose and Physical Health

Improved Longevity: Research has shown that individuals with a strong sense of purpose tend to live longer, healthier lives. Purpose provides a reason to wake up each morning, which can positively influence biological processes like heart health and immune function.

Healthy Habits: A purpose-driven life often encourages healthier choices. Whether it's eating well, exercising, or prioritizing rest, purposeful living fosters behaviors that enhance physical health.

4. Serving Others through Purpose

Connection and Community: Purpose often involves serving others, which strengthens relationships and builds a sense of belonging. This social connection is vital for emotional health and reduces feelings of loneliness.

Positive Ripple Effect: When you live purposefully, you inspire others to do the same. This creates a cycle of mutual growth and fulfillment, enriching the lives of everyone around you.

5. Living a Healthy Life Through Purpose

Aligning Actions with Values: Purposeful living encourages you to evaluate your priorities and focus on what truly matters. This mindfulness fosters balance, reducing burnout and improving mental health.

Joy in Contribution: Contributing to something greater than yourself gives life an irreplaceable richness. Whether it's helping others, pursuing a dream, or building something meaningful, the act of giving energizes and uplifts you.

Practical Tips to Embrace Purpose

1. Reflect on Your Passions: What makes you come alive? What problems do you feel compelled to solve?

2. Set Meaningful Goals: Break your purpose into actionable steps that guide your daily life.

3. Practice Gratitude: Recognize the impact your purpose has on others and your well-being.

4. Stay Flexible: Purpose evolves. Embrace growth and new opportunities to serve.

5. Cultivate a Faith-Based Approach: For faith-driven individuals, aligning purpose with God's plan brings deeper peace and direction.

When you live in alignment with your purpose, you experience a profound sense of happiness and health. Purpose lights the path toward a life filled with meaning, resilience, and joy.

To live a more fulfilled life, it's essential to find something that you are truly passionate about and dedicate yourself to it wholeheartedly. This doesn't always have to be something grand or monumental. Sometimes, it's the small things that bring the most joy.

Purpose beyond the ordinary

Our passions often lie in the things that bring us peace, joy, and fulfillment, even when the world is busy with demands and distractions. For me, one of the most fulfilling parts of my life has been the opportunity to serve others, particularly women. I am deeply passionate about uplifting and empowering women, which is why I started my youtube channel -Faith's Girlfriend series.

Even after a long and exhausting day at work, when I sit down to record episodes for my channel, something magical happens. All the fatigue melts away. The camera becomes my outlet, and I find myself energized, ready to share my thoughts, wisdom, and experiences with others. I can stay up late, recording and planning new content, because my purpose fills me with passion and joy.

Purpose gives you energy.

When you are in alignment with your purpose, you feel more alive. It's as if you tap into a well of energy that never runs dry. The work may be challenging, but it never feels like a burden. The passion you feel for what you're doing fuels you in ways that a regular task never could. This is the power of purpose—when you're doing what you love, the exhaustion of the day fades away, and you're filled with a renewed sense of energy and determination.

I know that when I am recording videos for my YouTube channel or helping women realize their potential, I feel a profound sense of fulfillment. It's the kind of joy that doesn't come from external rewards but from knowing I'm living out my purpose. The purpose that aligns with my passions gives me strength, joy, and perseverance.

Finding your purpose

If you want to experience true joy and fulfillment, it's crucial to find your purpose. This doesn't necessarily mean having a grand plan for your life right away. Sometimes, it's about identifying those small, meaningful moments that bring you joy—like baking a cake, helping a friend, or finding a way to serve others. Your purpose might evolve, but the key is to start somewhere. Find what makes you come alive, what energizes you, and follow that spark.

Ask yourself:

What brings me joy?

What can I do that makes a difference in the lives of others?

What makes me lose track of time because I am so deeply engaged in it?

When you can answer these questions, you are on your way to discovering your purpose.

Living your purpose

Living your purpose is about finding meaning in what you do, even in the most mundane moments. Purpose will give you the courage to push through hard times and the strength to celebrate your successes. It's a reminder that each day, no matter how tiring or stressful, is an opportunity to move closer to something that deeply matters to you.

For me, I have found that serving women, helping them discover their own passions, and sharing my story gives me the most satisfaction. No matter what else is happening in my life, I know that when I'm living out my purpose, I am on the right path.

Conclusion

When you live with purpose, you live with energy, fulfillment, and joy. The passion for what you do will infuse every moment, even the exhausting ones. Whether it's baking cakes for your children or helping others find their path, purpose makes every action meaningful.

So, I encourage you to take some time to reflect and ask yourself: What is my purpose? The answer may not come overnight, but when you start living with purpose, you'll know it's worth the pursuit. Find your purpose, live it out, and experience a life full of joy and fulfillment.

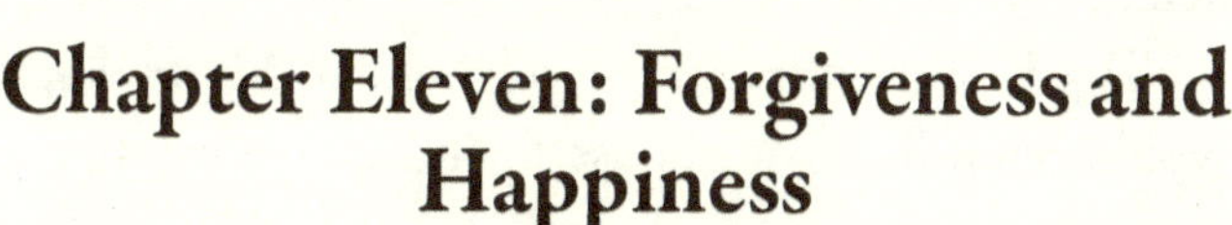

Chapter Eleven: Forgiveness and Happiness

"I would rather forgive than carry the load of unforgiveness"

Another crucial key to living a happy life is learning to forgive. When we walk around harboring bitterness and anger, happiness becomes impossible to attain. Forgiveness is not just a gift to others—it is a gift to yourself, freeing your heart from the heavy chains of resentment.

One of the most profound lessons I've learned about forgiveness came from one of my best friends, Mercy. She is, without a doubt, the most forgiving person I know, and her unwavering commitment to this virtue has had a lasting impact on my life.

We once worked together under a boss who could only be described as difficult. His actions, whether intentional or not, seemed designed to cause pain or frustration. While the rest of us struggled with resentment and avoided speaking to him, Mercy took a different approach. Every morning, she would walk into the office, and greet him warmly with a smile while the rest of us struggled with being cordial.

I remember being amazed by her ability to let go and forgive. While I harbored anger and bitterness, Mercy was free. She didn't allow unforgiveness or negativity to take root in her heart. Watching her live her life with such grace taught me that forgiveness isn't just about the other person—it's about liberating yourself from the burden of anger.

Forgiveness in action:

Another profound example of forgiveness that has deeply influenced me is my mother. When she married into my father's family, she faced immense challenges. The family was not the easiest to deal with, and they gave her a very hard time. Despite their harsh treatment, my mother chose to love them. She chose to forgive them and move forward in peace.

I remember during the August holidays in primary school we would go to our village for the entire three-week holiday. My uncles, aunts, and cousins would often be at our house for breakfast, lunch, and supper. Despite all the past mistreatment and the pain they had caused her, I never once heard my mother complain. She never asked, "Why are they coming here? After all the hurt they've caused me?" No, she simply forgave them and welcomed them with an open heart.

This has always stood out to me as a constant reminder that no matter how people treat me, I do not have to respond in the same way. I have the power to choose forgiveness. I can choose to be better, to take the higher road, and to release bitterness and anger. My mother's ability to forgive and embrace others has been a life lesson I carry with me every day. Even now, she remains one of the most remarkable women I know when it comes to the art of forgiveness.

Her example of unconditional love and forgiveness has taught me that true freedom comes from letting go of grudges. It's a choice—one that not only heals others but also frees our hearts to live in peace and joy. I am forever grateful to have such a powerful role model in my life.

Bitterness and happiness cannot coexist.

As a wife, a parent, a sister, a daughter, an employee, or an employer, you will encounter situations that hurt, disappoint, or frustrate you. However, bitterness and happiness cannot coexist in the same heart. The more space you give to anger and resentment, the less room you leave for peace, joy, and love. Forgiveness is the pathway to reclaiming your happiness.

I learned this valuable lesson early in life. The word of god teaches us to forgive others. In the lord's prayer, we say, "Forgive us our trespasses, as we forgive those who trespass against us." This means that if I desire forgiveness from god and those around me, I must first extend forgiveness to others.

Forgiveness: A biblical mandate

The Bible is filled with scriptures that emphasize the importance of forgiveness. Ephesians 4:31-32 says, "Get rid of all bitterness, rage, and anger, brawling and slander, along with every form of malice. Be kind and compassionate to one another, forgiving each other, just as in christ god forgave you."

Forgiveness is not an option—it is a mandate. By forgiving, we emulate Christ, who forgave us even when we were undeserving. Holding on to unforgiveness is like drinking poison and expecting the other person to suffer. It only harms you and robs you of the joy that god desires for you.

Letting go of pain

To forgive is to release the pain and negativity that weigh you down. It means refusing to carry the burden of someone else's wrongdoing into your future. Forgiveness does not mean condoning the offense or forgetting the hurt. Instead, it means choosing to let go of the anger and allowing healing to take place.

Think about it: How often do we carry resentment toward people who may not even realize they have hurt us? While we brood over their actions, they continue with their lives, oblivious to the turmoil they've caused. Why should we let them steal our joy? Forgiveness is not for their benefit—it is for ours.

Forgiveness in Relationships

Forgiveness is essential in every relationship—be it with your spouse, children, siblings, parents, friends, or colleagues. As humans, we are imperfect, and conflicts are inevitable. However, if we cling to every slight or wrong, we will only build walls instead of bridges.

In marriage, for instance, forgiveness is a daily decision. No matter how much you love your spouse, misunderstandings will arise. Holding on to grudges creates a toxic environment that stifles joy and peace.

Forgiveness, on the other hand, restores harmony and allows love to thrive.

In our relationships with siblings and parents, unresolved grievances can fester for years, robbing us of the joy of family. We must learn to let go, to extend grace as we have received grace, and to prioritize love over pride.

Practical steps to forgive

1. Acknowledge the pain: Recognize the hurt and allow yourself to feel it. Forgiveness is not about suppressing emotions but processing them in a healthy way.

2. Pray for strength: Ask god to help you forgive, especially when it feels impossible. Philippians 4:13 reminds us, "I can do all things through Christ who strengthens me."

3. Let go of the offense: Release the desire for revenge or retribution. Trust that god is the ultimate judge and will handle the situation according to his justice and mercy.

4. Seek reconciliation, if possible: When appropriate, communicate with the person who hurt you. Share your feelings and work toward mending the relationship.

5. Focus on the future: Do not dwell on past hurts. Instead, choose to move forward with hope and peace in your heart.

The freedom of forgiveness

When you choose forgiveness, you choose freedom. You release yourself from the bondage of anger and resentment, allowing joy and peace to fill your heart. Forgiveness does not mean you forget the hurt, but it means the hurt no longer controls you.

At the end of your life, what will you want to look back on? A life spent nurturing bitterness, or a life filled with love, peace, and happiness? Don't carry resentment to your grave. Instead, let go, forgive, and live fully. As Matthew 6:14-15 reminds us, "If you forgive others their trespasses, your heavenly Father will also forgive you, but if you do not forgive others their trespasses, neither will your Father forgive your trespasses."

Conclusion

Forgiveness is a powerful tool for living a happy and fulfilling life. It frees you from the chains of bitterness, restores broken relationships, and aligns your heart with god's will. Remember, forgiving others is not a sign of weakness—it is a testament to your strength and faith. Choose forgiveness, and you will find that happiness is no longer elusive but ever-present in your life.

Chapter Twelve: The Role of Faith

As a born-again Christian, my faith has been the bedrock of my happiness and joy. It has taught me the power of surrender, trust, and hope in a higher power. Through faith, I have learned to cast my burdens on Christ, finding solace and peace in his unchanging love and promises.

Faith is a powerful force in shaping our lives, and it plays a critical role in our happiness. For many, faith is not just about believing in something greater than ourselves; it is a source of strength, hope, and purpose. The scriptures provide us with timeless wisdom and guidance that can help us cultivate lasting joy, regardless of our circumstances. This chapter explores the role of faith in fostering happiness and how we can use scripture to nourish our spirits, trust in god's plan, and find peace and joy in all seasons of life.

Faith as the foundation of true happiness

True happiness is not dependent on external circumstances—it comes from within, grounded in our faith and trust in god. Scriptures remind us that happiness is deeply rooted in our relationship with god and his promises. The foundation of lasting joy is not based on fleeting emotions or material achievements but on the assurance that god is with us, guiding us through every challenge and blessing.

Philippians 4:4-7 reminds us of the power of faith in bringing peace and joy into our lives:

"Rejoice in the Lord always. I will say it again: Rejoice! Let your gentleness be evident to all. The Lord is near. Do not be anxious about anything, but in every situation, by prayer and petition, with thanksgiving, present your requests to god. And the peace of god, which transcends all understanding, will guard your hearts and your minds in christ Jesus."

This passage emphasizes that through rejoicing in the lord and trusting him with our worries, we receive peace—peace that guards our hearts and minds. Faith and trust in god lay the groundwork for happiness, reminding us that joy is a choice, even in difficult times.

Faith provides a source of hope.

Hope is a key element of happiness, and faith gives us the hope to persevere through life's challenges. When we have faith in god's promises, we know that we are never alone and that there is a purpose behind every season we go through. In times of hardship or uncertainty, our faith provides the hope that things will get better and that god is working all things together for our good.

Romans 15:13 says:

"May the god of hope fill you with all joy and peace as you trust in him, so that you may overflow with hope by the power of the holy spirit."

This verse shows us that as we trust in god, we are filled with joy, peace, and hope. Faith anchors our souls and allows us to experience a deep sense of contentment, regardless of our circumstances. Hope in god's promises leads us to a place of joy and fulfillment that the world cannot take away.

Faith enables us to overcome worry and anxiety.

In today's world, anxiety and worry can often steal our peace and happiness. However, the scriptures teach us that we do not need to carry the burden of anxiety alone. Through faith, we can release our worries to god, trusting that he cares for us and will provide for our needs.

Matthew 6:25-34 speaks powerfully about the importance of trusting god to meet our needs and free us from anxiety:

"Therefore I tell you, do not worry about your life, what you will eat or drink; or about your body, what you will wear. Is not life more than food, and the body more than clothes? ... But seek first his kingdom and his righteousness, and all these things will be given to you as well."

This passage teaches us to focus on god's kingdom and his righteousness, not on the worries and distractions of life. By doing so, we are assured that god will take care of our needs, giving us the peace of mind to enjoy life's blessings without being overwhelmed by anxiety.

Faith helps us build resilience in the face of trials.

Life is full of challenges, but faith helps us navigate through them with resilience and joy. Instead of viewing difficulties as obstacles that will defeat us, we can look at them through the lens of faith, knowing that god is using these moments to refine and strengthen us.

James 1:2-4 offers valuable guidance on finding joy in trials:

"Consider it pure joy, my brothers and sisters, whenever you face trials of many kinds, because you know that the testing of your faith produces perseverance. Let perseverance finish its work so that you may be mature and complete, not lacking anything."

This scripture encourages us to consider trials as opportunities for growth. While it's natural to feel pain and frustration during challenging times, faith gives us the perspective that our perseverance and trust in god's plan will lead us to maturity and spiritual completeness. This perspective not only helps us cope but also enables us to find joy even amid difficulties.

Faith helps us appreciate the blessings we have

Faith helps us shift our focus from what we don't have to what we do have. When we place our trust in god, we learn to be content in all circumstances, appreciating the blessings in our lives rather than longing for more. Gratitude is a key component of happiness, and faith helps us cultivate a grateful heart.

1 thessalonians 5:16-18 advises:

"Rejoice always, pray continually, give thanks in all circumstances; for this is god's will for you in christ Jesus."

Gratitude transforms our perspective and fills us with joy. By choosing to give thanks to god in all circumstances, we recognize the many gifts he has given us—our health, our relationships, our purpose—and we grow in appreciation for the beauty of life.

The power of prayer and meditation

Faith in god also brings us closer to him through prayer and meditation, which are powerful tools for cultivating happiness. Prayer allows us to pour out our hearts to god, find peace in his presence, and receive guidance. Through prayer, we connect with the creator who understands our deepest needs and desires.

Psalm 46:10 says:

"Be still, and know that I am god."

This simple yet profound command reminds us to pause, reflect, and trust that god is in control. In the stillness of prayer and meditation, we find peace, joy, and clarity, helping us to align our hearts with god's will for our lives.

Finding strength in god's love

On days when I wake up feeling low, overwhelmed, or ungrateful, I remind myself of the love Christ has for me. The knowledge that he chose to die for me—a sacrifice born out of immense love—fills me with gratitude and lifts my spirit. This love, so pure and unconditional, is a constant reminder that I am valued, cherished, and never alone.

When life gets tough, whether it's in my marriage, friendships, or personal challenges, my faith becomes my refuge. If my husband and I are in disagreement or facing challenges, I know I can turn to god in prayer. I lay my burdens at his feet, trusting him to bring healing, clarity, and peace. This act of surrender has brought me immense relief and joy, knowing I don't have to carry the weight of the world on my shoulders.

Hope for a brighter tomorrow

Faith gives me a deep assurance that no matter how challenging today might be, tomorrow holds the promise of something better. The word of god is filled with promises that encourage me to hold on, to trust that his plans are good and full of hope.

Jeremiah 29:11 reminds me:

"For I know the plans I have for you," Declares the lord, "plans to prosper you and not to harm you, plans to give you a future and a hope."

This scripture, along with many others, has been an anchor in my life. It keeps me grounded during storms and helps me rise above the waves of worry or despair.

The joy of casting burdens on Christ

The Bible calls us to "cast all your anxieties on him because he cares for you" (1 Peter 5:7). This verse has been a guide for me, teaching me to release control and trust in god's ability to handle every situation. Whether it's family disagreements, career challenges, or personal struggles, I've learned that prayer is a powerful tool to offload stress and gain perspective.

Faith for those seeking joy

If you're not a person of faith, I encourage you to seek it out. Faith isn't about religion; it's about building a relationship with god. It's about finding a source of strength, hope, and peace that transcends human understanding.

Here's how you can start:

1. Seek god in prayer: Open your heart to him. Speak honestly about your fears, struggles, and hopes.

2. Read the word: Start with the psalms or the gospels. The bible is a treasure trove of wisdom, comfort, and encouragement.

3. Connect with a faith community: Surround yourself with people who share a belief in god's love and promises. Their support can be invaluable in your journey.

4. Be patient: Faith is a journey. Allow yourself time to grow in understanding and trust.

Conclusion: Faith as the path to lasting happiness

Faith is a powerful tool for cultivating happiness because it grounds us in the belief that our joy is not dependent on external circumstances, but on the assurance that god loves us and is working in our lives. By trusting in god's promises, releasing anxiety, building resilience through trials, and practicing gratitude, we can experience lasting happiness.

The scriptures provide us with the wisdom to live a joyful life—one rooted in faith, hope, and love. When we rely on god and trust in his plan for our lives, our happiness becomes a reflection of his goodness and faithfulness. Remember, your joy comes not from what you have or don't have, but from your trust in the one who created you and loves you unconditionally.

Chapter thirteen : Gratitude

As we conclude on our journey to happiness thre some recurring themes I believe you have come across in the book which I believe I would also like to reempasize again. Its important that we understand the relationship between gratitude and living a healthier, happier life, below are some key insights:

1. Gratitude and Mental Health

Reduces Negative Emotions: Gratitude has been shown to reduce feelings of envy, resentment, and regret while increasing optimism and positivity. This mental shift fosters a healthier emotional state.

Protects Against Depression: Regular gratitude practices can serve as a natural buffer against depressive symptoms, making it an effective supplement to traditional treatments for mental health challenges.

2. Impact on Physical Health

Improved Heart Health: Grateful individuals often report lower blood pressure and better heart function. For example, gratitude practices have been linked to recovery from coronary events.

Better Sleep Quality: Reflecting on gratitude before bed can lead to deeper, more restorative sleep.

Boosted Immunity: Gratitude is linked to lower levels of stress hormones like cortisol, which helps in strengthening the immune system.

3. Gratitude and Social Connections

Stronger Relationships: Expressing gratitude helps build and maintain social bonds, creating a network of support and fostering mutual trust.

Improved Conflict Resolution: Gratitude encourages empathy and reduces the likelihood of engaging in destructive communication.

4. Long-term Happiness

Sustained Joy: Unlike fleeting pleasures, gratitude fosters long-term happiness by helping individuals focus on the good in their lives rather than what's lacking.

Encourages a Growth Mindset: By highlighting personal strengths and blessings, gratitude fosters resilience in facing challenges.

5. Practical Benefits of Gratitude

Enhanced Productivity: Gratitude improves focus and motivation, making individuals more effective at work and in daily tasks.

Promotes Generosity: Grateful individuals are more likely to help others, creating a positive feedback loop of giving and receiving.

6. Scientific Backing

Neurobiological Changes: Gratitude activates the brain's reward system, increasing dopamine and serotonin levels, which are critical for happiness and emotional regulation.

Habit Formation: Practicing gratitude rewires the brain to focus on positives, making optimism a default state over time.

7. Ways to Practice Gratitude

Keeping a gratitude journal.

Expressing appreciation to others through notes or verbal acknowledgment.

Mindful reflection or prayer focusing on blessings.

Participating in gratitude challenges or apps that encourage daily reflection.

Here's a structured guide to help you incorporate gratitude into your daily life for better mental and emotional well-being:

Daily Gratitude Practice Guide

1. Start Your Day with Gratitude

Morning Reflection: Spend 2–3 minutes reflecting on three things you're thankful for before getting out of bed.

Gratitude Affirmations: Repeat positive affirmations like, "I am grateful for the opportunities today brings."

2. Keep a Gratitude Journal

What to Write: Each evening, list at least three things you are grateful for that day. Be specific (e.g., "I'm thankful for the 30-minute walk I had this morning").

Reflect: Write why each item matters to you and how it positively impacts your life.

3. Practice Gratitude Meditation

Duration: Dedicate 5–10 minutes daily to focus on your blessings.

How: Close your eyes, breathe deeply, and visualize the people, experiences, or achievements you're thankful for.

4. Express Gratitude to Others

Daily Acknowledgments: Make it a habit to thank at least one person daily, either in person, via text, or with a handwritten note.

Highlight Their Impact: Be specific about what you appreciate about them.

5. Turn Challenges into Opportunities for Gratitude

Reframe Negative Events: For any challenging situation, ask yourself, "What can I learn from this?" or "What am I still grateful for despite this challenge?"

Celebrate Progress: Focus on small victories during tough times.

6. Use Visual Reminders

Gratitude Jar: Keep a jar where you write down one gratitude on a small note daily. Review them monthly or when you need a positivity boost.

Vision Board: Create a board displaying images or quotes that remind you of what you value and are grateful for.

7. Leverage Technology

Gratitude Apps: Use apps like Grateful or Day One Journal to write down what you are grateful for.

Daily Reminders: Set a phone reminder to pause and think about one thing you're thankful for.

8. Involve Others

Family Gratitude Practice: During meals or gatherings, ask everyone to share one thing they're grateful for.

Gratitude Groups: Join or create a community where members share weekly reflections on gratitude.

9. Reflect on Long-term Blessings

Take time weekly to think about big-picture blessings, such as your health, relationships, or personal growth.

Reflect on how past challenges shaped you into a stronger person.

Tracking Progress

Revisit your journal entries monthly to see how your mindset has evolved.

Track improvements in your mood, relationships, and overall satisfaction with life.

I found that there is substantial evidence linking gratitude practices, such as writing down daily what we are thankful for, with a positive attitude and increased happiness.

1. Enhanced Happiness and Emotional Well-being: Studies show that individuals who regularly document things they are grateful for experience higher levels of happiness and satisfaction. For example, Emmons and McCullough's 2003 research found that people who practiced gratitude journaling reported greater optimism and positivity compared to those who focused on negative experiences or were in a neutral group. The gratitude group also experienced fewer physical complaints and improved life satisfaction.

2. Reduction in Stress and Depression: Gratitude journaling has been shown to reduce depressive symptoms significantly, sometimes by as much as 35% during the journaling period. It also helps in managing stress, particularly in high-pressure environments like healthcare settings, as demonstrated in various studies.

3. Improved Physical Health and Sleep: Regular gratitude practices can lead to better sleep quality, reduced blood pressure, and a stronger

immune system. People who maintain a gratitude journal also tend to exercise more frequently, contributing to their overall well-being.

4. Positive Social and Psychological Impact: Gratitude enhances social bonds and reduces feelings of envy, fostering a more positive outlook on life. This ripple effect strengthens relationships and contributes to a more supportive social environment, further boosting happiness.

Incorporating a daily gratitude practice, such as writing down three things you're thankful for, is a simple yet effective way to cultivate a more positive mindset and improve overall well-being.

As we start off on this journey lets start by practicing gratitude and contentment to foster happiness.

Here's a sample gratitude prompt:

Today, I am thankful for...

1. ....

2. ....

3. ....

Gratitude is a practice that has the potential to significantly enhance our mental, emotional, and physical well-being. Research consistently shows that individuals who make a habit of expressing gratitude—whether through journaling, affirmations, or daily reflections—experience a greater sense of happiness, reduced stress, and improved relationships. Moreover, expressing gratitude not only nurtures our own sense of contentment but also creates a ripple effect that strengthens social bonds and cultivates a sense of community. By embedding gratitude into daily routines, we lay the foundation for a happier, healthier, and more fulfilling life.

Ending the Journey: Embracing Happiness

As we conclude this journey together, remember that happiness is not a destination, but a choice—a state of mind we must continually nurture. Life will always present challenges, but our response to them shapes our experience. The pursuit of happiness is not about avoiding struggles or finding a perfect life; it's about choosing to find happiness, even in the midst of adversity.

Throughout this book, we've explored the importance of self-love, the power of gratitude, giving, power of purpose and role faith plays in our ability to live happy lives. These are not just concepts but practices that require our intentional effort each day. By embracing these principles, we take control of our own happiness, regardless of external circumstances.

Happiness begins with you. It's not something that happens to you, but something you create through your thoughts, actions, and choices. As you go forward, let go of the limiting beliefs that hold you back and make space for the abundance of joy that life has to offer. Remember, you deserve happiness, and by prioritizing your well-being, you not only improve your life but also inspire those around you to do the same.

So, choose happiness today. Live with purpose, embrace your imperfections, and keep choosing joy. As you walk this path, may you find peace in knowing that, above all, I would rather be happy is not just a wish—it's a powerful affirmation that can transform your life.

About the Author

Faith is a devoted wife, a loving mother, a dedicated daughter, and an inspiring leader. With a thriving career and a passion for making a difference, she embodies the balance of personal and professional life. As a leader, she empowers those around her to achieve their best, while as a mother and wife, she cherishes the joy of nurturing her family.

Her journey has been shaped by a conscious decision to embrace happiness, finding joy in both the big and small moments of life. Through her experiences, she inspires others to prioritize self-love, gratitude, and purpose. In her book, I Would Rather Be Happy, she shares her insights and practical wisdom, encouraging readers to make the same powerful choice to live a life filled with happiness and fulfillment.

About the Author

Faith is a devoted wife, a loving mother, a dedicated daughter, and an inspiring leader. With a thriving career and a passion for making a difference, she embodies the balance of personal and professional life. As a leader, she empowers those around her to achieve their best, while as a mother and wife, she cherishes the joy of nurturing her family.

Her journey has been shaped by a conscious decision to embrace happiness, finding joy in both the big and small moments of life. Through her experiences, she inspires others to prioritize self-love, gratitude, and purpose. In her book, I'd Rather Be Happy, she shares her insights and practical wisdom, encouraging readers to make the same powerful choice to live a life filled with happiness and fulfillment.

www.ingramcontent.com/pod-product-compliance
Lightning Source LLC
LaVergne TN
LVHW040951150826
845672LV00002B/641

* 9 7 9 8 2 3 0 2 7 1 9 8 7 *